Winter Warmer

2025

Charlie Ellingworth

Copyright © 2025 Charlie Ellingworth

ISBN: 978-1-918424-02-7

PublishNation
www.publishnation.co.uk

There went out a decree from Rachel Reeves that all businesses should be taxed to fix the NHS. 'Tell me about it,' thought Joseph as his wife gave birth in a stable because there was no room for them in the maternity wing. Nearby, there were shepherds keeping watch over their flock by night because they couldn't rely on the police. And lo, a spokesman for the government came upon them, saying: "Fear not, for we are here to fix the foundations. And they were sore afraid.
Gordon Letherbridge adapting Luke 2

I certainly believe we all suffer damage, one way or another. How could we not, except in a world of perfect parents, siblings, neighbours, companions? And then there is the question, on which so much depends, of how we react to the damage: whether we admit it or repress it, and how this affects our dealings with others. Some admit the damage and try to mitigate it; some spend their lives trying to help others who are damaged; and then there are those whose main concern is to avoid further damage to themselves, at whatever cost. And those are the ones who are ruthless, and the ones to be careful of.
Julian Barnes: A Sense of an Ending

Marcus Aurelius without the philosophy.
Tom Holland on Keir Starmer.

Never heard of her.
A participant in a focus group when asked for their opinion on Mel Stride.

Are these real names?
Another participant - this time on Kemi Badenoch.

You should not be afraid of someone who has a library and reads many books; you should fear someone who has only one book; and he considers it sacred, but he has never read it.
Nietzsche

The food here is terrible, and the portions are so small!
Woody Allen

What every prime minister wants, fundamentally, is to be tasked with divvying up the proceeds of growth. All recent incumbents, though, have instead had to allocate the costs of decline.
Hugo Rifkind

The great thing to remember is that things aren't as bad as they were in the 14th century
Tom Holland

People say John Prescott made an impact on Britain. He certainly made an impact on me: a series of vigorous jabs to the chest as, late one night in a deserted Labour conference in corridor, he called me an effing bastard, saying he would "get me" in a spate of fruity language which visibly shocked the young civil servants around him. Although I was political editor of the BBC at the time and had just reported on the conference for the late-night news, I was confused. I couldn't remember anything I'd said that could have produced such a volcanic response from the deputy prime minister. He charged off again. I stood there, silently puzzling. Then he suddenly emerged from round another corner, put a hand on my shoulder and said, "sorry about that... wrong bloke."
Andrew Marr

Preach the Gospel always. If necessary, with words.
Francis of Assisi

When women gossip, we get called bitchy, but when men do it's called a podcast.
Sikisa Bostwick-Barnes

How can they tell?
Dorothy Parker – on being told that President Calvin Coolidge was dead

I shall be an autocrat: that's my trade. And the good Lord will forgive me: that's his.
Catherine the Great

The subject is something secondary. What I want to reproduce is what lies between the subject and me.
Monet

One problem is that a link between Christianity and liberalism exists only in branches of the religion. Eastern Orthodoxy has never promoted freedom of conscience in the manner of post-Reformation Christendom. Even in Western Christianity the connection is not universal. Toleration emerged in countries that rejected the authority of the Catholic Church over the inner life. Tellingly, it is in these countries – particularly in the Anglosphere – that woke movements have become most powerful. Woke – or, as it is more accurately described, hyper-liberalism – is a radical secular avatar of Christianity, in which the Protestant affirmation of personal autonomy in matters of belief has morphed into the assertion that truth is subjective.
John Gray

Cancellation in ancient Rome tended to involve more lions.
Steven Moffat

Desire makes everything blossom; possession makes everything wither and fade.
Proust

Ed Yong's An Immense World is about how animals perceive the world: there is something fascinating on every page. Here he describes the interplay between vision and colour - and which came first.

In 1992, Lars Chittka and Randolf Menzel analyzed 180 flowers and worked out what kind of eye would be best at discriminating their colors. The answer—an eye with green, blue, and UV trichromacy—is exactly what bees and many other insects have. You might think that these pollinators evolved eyes that see flowers well, but that's not what happened. Their style of trichromacy evolved hundreds of millions of years before the first flowers appeared, so the latter must have evolved to suit the former. Flowers evolved colours that ideally tickle insect eyes. I find these connections profound, in a way that makes me think differently about the act of sensing itself. Sensing can feel passive, as if eyes and other sense organs were intake valves through which animals absorb and receive the stimuli around them. But over time, the simple act of seeing recolours the world. Guided by evolution, eyes are living paintbrushes. Flowers, frogs, fish, feathers, and fruit all show that sight affects what is seen, and that much of what we find beautiful in nature has been shaped by the vision of our fellow animals. Beauty is not only in the eye of the beholder. It arises because of that eye.

If you press me to say why I loved him, I can say no more than because it was he, because it was I.
Montaigne - on his deep friend Etienne de la Boetie whose early death affected him for life.

There is a strange paradox that liberals are illiberal in their demand for liberality. They are exclusive in their demand for inclusivity and homogeneous in their demand for heterogeneity. They are somehow undiverse in their call for diversity. You can be diverse but not diverse in your opinions, your language or your behaviour.
Stephen Fry debating political correctness

It has been said that a pretty face is a passport. But it's not, it's a visa, and it runs out fast.
Julie Burchill

A precondition for reading good books is not reading bad ones: for life is short.
Schopenhauer

A good opening and a good ending make for a good film, as long as they come close together.
Fellini

He who feared that he would not succeed sat still.
Horace

Like space, the past is always nearer than we think. As a boy, I knew a woman who once cut Thomas Hardy's hair. For his part, Hardy knew an old countryman who had set eyes on Napoleon when the Bellerophon put into Plymouth Sound, en route to St Helena. The Napoleonic Wars are just three human lifetimes away and if you get to my age you will know that a lifetime is no vast span. Anthropologists have a thing called the 'long generation' - the era extending from the birth of one person to the death of the latest-born person that he or she could have met. This is where it gets hair-raising. As James Hawes puts it, in the foreword to his exhilarating The Shortest History of England (2021), 'Seven long generations ... the old and the young holding hands - and we are back at the Battle of Hastings.' This inspires the same sort of vertigo as the knowledge that standing in central London you are nearer to outer space than you are to, say, Market Harborough.
From a review of James Hawes's Shortest History of England. I was born in Market Harborough: who knew it was that close to heaven?

The term Republican or Democrat is irrelevant. Their old categorisations don't matter. You're either a populist nationalist or a global elitist.
Steve Bannon

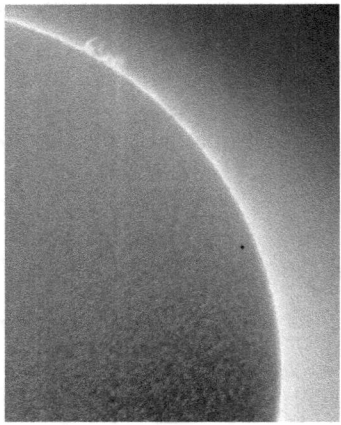

A photograph taken from the NASA probe within 3.5 million miles of the Sun's surface on Christmas Eve 2024. The black dot is Mercury.

Just typed 'manoeuvre' correctly on the first attempt, without even thinking about it. There are no worlds left to conquer.
J. K. Rowling. There are some worlds: diarrhoea.

An argument is made that there are just too many question marks about the near future; wouldn't it be better to wait until things clear up a bit? Before reaching for that crutch, face up to two unpleasant facts: The future is never clear; and you pay a very high price in the stock market for a cheery consensus. Uncertainty actually is the friend of the buyer of long-term values.
Warren Buffett

Any psychologist will tell you that boredom is subjective; it is a reflection of how we feel about an activity, and not a quality of the activity itself. As the psychologist Sandi Mann observes in

The Science of Boredom, Thomas Curwen, a scientist at Dulux responsible for studying how paint dries, loves his job. Watching paint dry can be fascinating, Curwen once told journalists, if you know how to look.
Sophie McBain in The New Statesman

If printing money could end poverty, printing diplomas would end stupidity.
Javier Milei

Only in Britain could it be thought a defect to be 'too clever by half'. The probability is that too many people are too stupid by three quarters.
John Major

I never apply the sword when the lash suffices, nor the lash when my tongue is enough. If there is even one thread binding me to my fellow man, I do not let it break. If he pulls, I loosen. If he loosens, I pull.
Muawiya, son-in-law of Mohammed and founder of the Umayyad dynasty.

Life, just like the stars, the planets and the galaxies, is just a temporary structure on the long road from order to disorder. But that doesn't make us insignificant, because we are the Cosmos made conscious. Life is the means by which the universe understands itself. And for me, our true significance lies in our ability to understand and explore this beautiful universe.
Brian Cox

I bring out the worst in my enemies, and that's how I get them to defeat themselves.
Roy Cohn, Donald Trump's mentor

A person's intelligence is directly reflected in the number of conflicting attitudes she can bring to bear on the same topic.
Lisa Alther

The further a society drifts from the truth, the more it will hate those who speak it.
Orwell

Sir,
My signal to my French partner, when he was over the top, was to say: "OK, Sean."And he would know to shut up because the French for bullshit is connerie.
Jenny Ray London N10: Letter to The Times

This was in my prayers: a measure of land not so large, with a garden and near the house a spring of pure water and in addition a little patch of woods. The gods have given me more and better. It is good. I ask for nothing more.
Horace

Easy reading is damn hard writing.
Nathaniel Hawthorne

In his new memoir, Just Different, the ballet dancer Wayne Sleep writes about being gay when it was illegal. He tells of one Covent Garden grandee who made his cottaging debut at the Waterloo station gents but didn't know the etiquette. When a note was passed under the partition asking what he enjoyed, he sent one back saying: "Maria Callas in Tosca."
Times Diary

The only difference between doctors and lawyers is that lawyers merely rob you, whereas doctors rob you and kill you too.
Chekhov. He knew of what he spoke; he was a doctor.

A bad lawyer is one who can make a case stretch on for ages. A good one can make it go on even longer.
Victoria Dowd (a lawyer)

And we pray, not
for new earth or heaven,
but to be quiet in heart,
and in eye clear.
What we need is here.
Wendell Berry

Oppression is what they do in the west. What they do in the
Middle East is their 'culture'.
Robert Harris

Our ordinary mind always tries to persuade us that we are
nothing but acorns and that our greatest happiness will be to
become bigger, fatter, shinier acorns; but that is of interest only
to pigs. Our faith gives us knowledge of something much
better: that we can become oak trees.
Ernst Schumacher

Punctuality is the courtesy of kings
Louis XVIII

I'm of the view that the reason for The Great Silence (why we
have not been contacted by extraterrestrial life) is that
civilisations are inevitably crushed by the weight of 'knobheads'
shortly after inventing the internet.
Professor Brian Cox

He either fears his fate too much,
Or his deserts are small,
That puts it not unto the touch
To win or lose it all
The Marquis of Montrose

Appears to be a gentleman, but you can't help feeling there's something hidden behind it all.
From Cambridge's Varsity magazine about Robert Jenrick.

I do miss the fact that they don't play a song when you walk into a room any more. I was lost for three weeks after I left office.
Bill Clinton on what he misses about being US president.

The desires of the heart are crooked as corkscrews.
Auden

Dads are supposed to be embarrassing but it is possible to overachieve.
Ed Balls on his time on Strictly Come Dancing

Twenty years at No 1, and not a single penny in royalties.
Eric Idle after Always Look on the Bright Side of Life dropped out of the top ten songs played at funerals.

I never lose sight of the fact that just being is fun.
Katharine Hepburn

Airplane travel is nature's way of making you look like your passport photo.
Al Gore

If you want your marriage to prosper like love in a loving cup
Whenever you're wrong admit it and whenever you're right shut up.
Ogden Nash

I wish what every addict wishes for: that what we love is good for us.
David Lynch on cigarettes

It's not that we have a short time to live, but that we waste a lot of it.
Seneca

Chloroform in print.
Mark Twain on the Book of Mormon

British men have fared very poorly in an international comparison of average penis size produced earlier this year. According to Worlddata, which reviewed 40 studies spanning 88 countries, the nation with the largest average erect penis length is Ecuador (6.9in), followed by Cameroon (6.56m) and Bolivia (6.5in).
The UK ranks 68th, with an average length of 5.16in. Almost "the only people we can feel superior around, when it comes to our trousers, are Cambodia and Yemen", lamented Caitlin Moran in The Times. "The rest of the world is putting on a sympathetic face and saying, 'But you have lovely eyes, Britain! And a kind heart!'"
The Week

Doris: You have no values in your life. It's nihilism, it's cynicism, it's sarcasm, and orgasm.
Woody Allen: Yeah, you know in France, I could run on that slogan and win.
Deconstructing Harry 1997

FROM: David Trott   23 August 2000

TERRITORIAL EFFECT

During a recent due diligence process underway at a Swiss client, the attached clause 10.4 was found embedded in one of their agreements. Nobody at the client has any recollection of involvement in the contract that was drafted but have asked me for my views on its effect. If anybody has any thoughts ....

```
     (f)  sixth, any excess to the Company.

     10.4    End of the World.  Upon the occurrence of the end of the
world before full payment and performance of the Notes and
Drafts, the Notes and Drafts, at the option of the Required
Banks, will become immediately due and payable in full and may be
enforced against the Company by any available terrestrial, extra
terrestrial or spiritual procedure.  For remedial purposes and
for purposes of determining the relative equities of the parties,
the Company, by virtue of its attorneys, will be deemed to be
aligned with the forces of light, and the Banks and their
attorneys will be deemed to be aligned with the forces of
darkness, regardless of actual ultimate terrestrial, extra
terrestrial or spiritual destinations of the Company or the banks
or any of their particular officers (including the Treasurer and
the Vice President-Finance).

     11.  WAIVERS, AMENDMENTS AND REMEDIES.

     11.1    Waivers and Remedies.  No delay or omission of the
Required Banks to exercise any right under the Loan Documents
shall impair such right or be construed to be a waiver of any
Event of Default or an acquiescence therein, and any single or
partial exercise of any such right shall not preclude other or
further exercise thereof or the exercise of any other right, and
no waiver, amendment or other variation of the terms, conditions
```

-16-

JG Ballard, the creator of Crash and Empire of the Sun and, in many ways, a new form of science fiction, had an unblinking view of humanity and modernity. This is the credo of an unsettling and surreal imagination.

I believe in the power of the imagination to remake the world, to release the truth within us, to hold back the night, to transcend death, to charm motorways, to ingratiate ourselves with birds, to enlist the confidences of madmen.
I believe in my own obsessions, in the beauty of the car crash, in the peace of the submerged forest, in the excitements of the deserted holiday beach, in the elegance of automobile graveyards, in the mystery of multi-storey car parks, in the poetry of abandoned hotels.

I believe in the forgotten runways of Wake Island, pointing towards the Pacifics of our imaginations.

I believe in the mysterious beauty of Margaret Thatcher, in the arch of her nostrils and the sheen on her lower lip; in the melancholy of wounded Argentine conscripts; in the haunted smiles of filling station personnel; in my dream of Margaret Thatcher caressed by that young Argentine soldier in a forgotten motel watched by a tubercular filling station attendant.

I believe in the beauty of all women, in the treachery of their imaginations, so close to my heart; in the junction of their disenchanted bodies with the enchanted chromium rails of supermarket counters; in their warm tolerance of my perversions.

I believe in the death of tomorrow, in the exhaustion of time, in our search for a new time within the smiles of auto-route waitresses and the tired eyes of air-traffic controllers at out-of-season airports.

I believe in the genital organs of great men and women, in the body postures of Ronald Reagan, Margaret Thatcher and Princess Di, in the sweet odours emanating from their lips as they regard the cameras of the entire world.

I believe in madness, in the truth of the inexplicable, in the common sense of stones, in the lunacy of flowers, in the disease stored up for the human race by the Apollo astronauts.

I believe in nothing.

I believe in Max Ernst, Delvaux, Dali, Titian, Goya, Leonardo, Vermeer, Chirico, Magritte, Redon, Duerer, Tanguy, the Facteur Cheval, the Watts Towers, Boecklin, Francis Bacon, and all the invisible artists within the psychiatric institutions of the planet.

I believe in the impossibility of existence, in the humour of mountains, in the absurdity of electromagnetism, in the farce of geometry, in the cruelty of arithmetic, in the murderous intent of logic.

I believe in adolescent women, in their corruption by their own leg stances, in the purity of their dishevelled bodies, in the traces of their pudenda left in the bathrooms of shabby motels.

I believe in flight, in the beauty of the wing, and in the beauty of everything that has ever flown, in the stone thrown by a small child that carries with it the wisdom of statesmen and midwives.

I believe in the gentleness of the surgeon's knife, in the limitless geometry of the cinema screen, in the hidden universe within supermarkets, in the loneliness of the sun, in the garrulousness of planets, in the repetitiveness or ourselves, in the inexistence of the universe and the boredom of the atom.

I believe in the light cast by video-recorders in department store windows, in the messianic insights of the radiator grilles of showroom automobiles, in the elegance of the oil stains on the engine nacelles of 747s parked on airport tarmacs.

I believe in the non-existence of the past, in the death of the future, and the infinite possibilities of the present.

I believe in the derangement of the senses: in Rimbaud, William Burroughs, Huysmans, Genet, Celine, Swift, Defoe, Carroll, Coleridge, Kafka.

I believe in the designers of the Pyramids, the Empire State Building, the Berlin Fuehrerbunker, the Wake Island runways.

I believe in the body odours of Princess Di.

I believe in the next five minutes.

I believe in the history of my feet.

I believe in migraines, the boredom of afternoons, the fear of calendars, the treachery of clocks.

I believe in anxiety, psychosis and despair.

I believe in the perversions, in the infatuations with trees, princesses, prime ministers, derelict filling stations (more beautiful than the Taj Mahal), clouds and birds.

I believe in the death of the emotions and the triumph of the imagination.

I believe in Tokyo, Benidorm, La Grande Motte, Wake Island, Eniwetok, Dealey Plaza.

I believe in alcoholism, venereal disease, fever and exhaustion.

I believe in pain.

I believe in despair.

I believe in all children.

I believe in maps, diagrams, codes, chess-games, puzzles, airline timetables, airport indicator signs.
I believe all excuses.
I believe all reasons.
I believe all hallucinations.
I believe all anger.
I believe all mythologies, memories, lies, fantasies, evasions.
I believe in the mystery and melancholy of a hand, in the kindness of trees, in the wisdom of light.
JG Ballard: What I believe

When we're young, everyone over the age of thirty looks middle-aged, everyone over fifty antique. And time, as it goes by, confirms that we weren't that wrong. Those little age differentials, so crucial and so gross when we are young, erode. We end up all belonging to the same category, that of the non-young.
Julian Barnes: Sense of an Ending

I cannot praise a fugitive and cloistered virtue, that never sallies out and sees her adversary.
Milton: Areopagitica

I'm a kind of hostage in my own life. My mind is always stealing away my joy. I've had 60 years of covering wars, revolutions, famines, earthquakes. When I put my head on the pillow at night, it all comes back and dances in front of me, saying, "You're not going to sleep. You're going to go back to the war where 600 children are coming at you thinking you're an aid worker and all you're bringing them is a Nikon camera around your neck.
Don McCullin

The old Saudi brand was 'austere theocracy', but the new one is 'fun, fun, fun, but still with beheading'
Helen Lewis in The Atlantic

Small, hurried steps like a partridge conscious of pursuit but reluctant to do anything so undignified as fly.
Matthew Parris describing Margaret Thatcher's walk

The meaning of life? Enjoying the passage of time. That's it. That's the whole thing. Think about it - the odds of us even existing are so impossibly small. Not just our parents meeting at the exact right moment, but their parents, and their parents before them, going all the way back through billions of years of evolution. One tiny change in that chain, and poof - we wouldn't be here. Yet somehow, we are. Breathing. Alive. Aware. Able to laugh, love, think, create, and feel the sun on our skin. We spend so much time chasing meaning, purpose, success - but maybe it's simpler than that. Maybe it's just about being present. Feeling the moments as they pass. Appreciating the absurd beauty of existing at all. Enjoying the passage of time. It's not everything, but it's enough.
Jimmy Carr

How do you know if a pass is unwanted until you've made it? I should have taken that to heart before I went to university. Foolish pride and a horror of importuning anyone has always stayed my hand. Silly, I know. When have I ever been hurt, or

thought the less of anyone, because they made a pass at me which I chose to decline? Mostly I've been flattered. If only I'd operated on the same principle as some of my friends: that if you chat up enough people, sooner or later you'll score.
Alan Clark

If they can put one man on the moon, why not all of them?

Feminist T-Shirt

More than a decade ago, Lawson developed early symptoms of progressive supranuclear palsy, a form of Parkinson's disease, so he moved to a spacious flat in Brighton overlooking the seafront, which he shared with his husband, Jamie Whittington, whom he had met in the mid-Eighties in Nassau, where Whittington was a croupier in a casino. Lawson was especially content with his life at this address, as there were no objects on the horizon coloured green, which was a colour he abhorred because it reminded him of nature and the countryside.
He liked his penthouse flat in Long Acre for the same reason. Lawson was baffled by friends who lived in the countryside, which he found static and boring compared with the variegated existence one could have in a city. He told his friend Kasmin that there was too much grass in the world and he didn't want to be reminded of it except when it was in the form of marijuana.
Times obituary of George Lawson, bookseller.

Many algorithmic biases share the same fundamental problem: the computer thinks it has discovered some truth about humans, when in fact it has imposed order on them. A social media algorithm thinks it has discovered that humans like outrage, when in fact it is the algorithm itself that conditioned humans to produce and consume more outrage. Such biases result, on the one hand, from the computers discounting the full spectrum of human abilities and, on the other hand, from the computers discounting their own power to influence humans. Even if computers observe that almost all humans behave in a particular way, it doesn't mean humans are bound to behave like that.

Maybe it just means that the computers themselves are rewarding such behaviour while punishing and blocking alternatives. For computers to have a more accurate and responsible view of the world, they need to take into account their own power and impact. And for that to happen, the humans who currently engineer computers need to accept that they are not manufacturing new tools. They are unleashing new kinds of independent agents, and potentially even new kinds of gods.
Novel Yuval Harari

After an attack by insurgents during the Malaya uprising in the 1950s, the British High Commissioner, Gerald Templer, roared into the village in a jeep, jumped out with his translator and gave the guerrillas a good tongue-lashing. "You are a bunch of bastards," he told them. "But let me tell you: I can be a bastard too." The translator duly conveyed this ominous message as: "None of your parents were married when you were born. But don't worry – mine weren't either."

Thoughts of his own death, like the distant roll of thunder at a picnic.
Auden: Prologue at Sixty,

It never troubles the wolf how many the sheep may be.
Virgil

For Aristotle and his successors, the substance of justice or goodness was as much a function of convention as of definition. Like pornography, these attributes might be impossible to define but you knew them when you saw them. The attractions of a 'reasonable' level of wealth, an 'acceptable' compromise, a just or good resolution were self-evident. The avoidance of extremes was a moral virtue in its own right, as well as a condition of political stability. However, the idea of moderation—so familiar to generations of moralists—is difficult to articulate today. Big is not always better, more not

always desirable; but we are discouraged from expressing the thought.
One source of our confusion may be a blurring of the distinction between law and justice. In the US especially, so long as a practice is not illegal we find it hard to define its shortcomings. The notion of 'prudence' eludes us: the idea that it is imprudent as well as improper for Goldman Sachs to distribute billions of dollars in less than a year after benefiting from taxpayer largesse would have been self-evident to men of the Scottish Enlightenment, just as it would to the classical philosophers. 'Imprudence' in this respect would have been as reprehensible as financial chicanery: not least for the risks to which it exposed the community at large.
Tony Judt: Ill Fares the Land

Pain is certain, suffering optional.

Buddha

The commentary on Israel/Gaza is rarely evenhanded or subtle. This, by a Jewish woman, is a rarity.

Some will roll their eyes. For God's sake, who cares about your nitpicking when tens of thousands of Palestinians have been killed? But since when did so many adults have such a zero-sum mentality? One can be horrified by Palestinian deaths and believe that Binyamin Netanyahu has been enabled for too long by too many in the West, while also acknowledging that Hamas is a murderous terrorist organisation and that Israel is and always has been surrounded by countries that want to destroy it. But holding more than one thought in one's head is too much to ask of too many people these days. So they say Israel is an evil colonialist country, an argument so simplistic and ludicrous that it was popularised first by 1950s Soviet Union propaganda. And now it is parroted by mainstream commentators on the left in the West.

Jews in this country have seen this coming for a while: the rise of "anti-zionism" as the socially acceptable form of antisemitism. Jeremy Corbyn was the canary in this septic coalmine, laying the groundwork for a new generation on the left to see Israel as a whole as bad, thereby greatly simplifying the narrative for itself when Hamas attacked. Again and again I read people comparing October 7 to a "slave uprising" — a reflection of the rise of identity politics, which sees everything through the prism of race.

Suddenly Hamas terrorists are noble American slaves fighting against their masters. But Charleston, South Carolina, in the 1820s has as little do with modern-day Palestine and Israel as the moon. Israelis and Palestinians have been doing terrible things to each other for a very long time. Only the bigoted, the ignorant and — to be blunt — the stupid justify one side and damn the other. And yet even though Hamas was transparent in its murderous intentions and acts on October 7, it won global hearts and minds. Western politicians may still side with Israel, but they are the older generation; the younger generation that has grown up in the era of Netanyahu and antiZionism and identity politics sees things very differently. How does the future look for Jews? Complicated.
Hadley Freeman

I'm the only person on British TV who doesn't use an autocue. You know why? If you're half-pissed and read the autocue you slur your words.
Nigel Farage

The most profound technologies are those that disappear. They weave themselves into the fabric of everyday life until they are indistinguishable from it.
Mark Weiser, 1991

Anybody who has ever worked for a large company knows that strange notions and illconceived "initiatives" blow through such institutions like rotten autumn leaves through a ruined cottage. Sheer novelty is often a recommendation in itself. Though many executives were doubtless sincere, I suspect that for some of those now eschewing DEI, the term didn't represent much more than another attractive buzzword in a corporate culture addicted to buzzwords. The upside to not really caring about

ideas is that it is relatively easy to slough off the bad ones when you have tired of them.
James Marriot

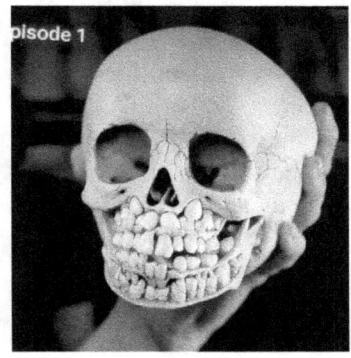

This is a young child's skull that shows its multiple layers of teeth. No wonder teething hurts so much.

A professor is one who talks in someone else's sleep.
WH Auden

Perhaps, in an age of populist promises, this is the cost. To win is to lie, and to serve is to disappoint.
Hugo Rifkind

If I had my time again, I would pay more regard to those poems of Horace which tell you you will not have your time again. Who knows how many tomorrows the gods will grant us? Now is the time, when you are young, to deck your hair with myrtle, drink the best of the wine, pluck the fruit.
Tom Stoppard: The Invention of Love

Samantha Harvey's Orbital won the Booker Prize last year. Many thought that a novella, with limited characterisation and little plot, about life in the Space Station, was an odd choice. Seen as a poetic meditation of beauty and insight, it was a worthy winner.

From up here in space where Roman glances out in passing through the dome of windows, the view is at first indistinct. It takes a moment to orientate. An expanse of wintry nothingness, pearly cloud cover, and then the familiar gleam of ice-sheet sloping off the Antarctic Circle. Starboard, the Seven Sisters audaciously bright. Sometimes there are urges to see a particular thing – the Pyramids or the New Zealand fjords or a desert of sand dunes that are bright orange and entirely abstract and which the eye can't fathom – the image could just as easily be a close-up of one of the heart cells they have in their Petri dishes. Sometimes they want to see the theatrics, the opera, the earth's atmosphere, airglow, and sometimes it's the smallest things, the lights of fishing boats off the coast of Malaysia dotted starlike in the black ocean. But now Roman can begin to see what he suspected was there, a thing they all know, with a kind of sixth sense, is there – the flexing, morphing green and red of the auroras which snake around the inside of the atmosphere fretful and magnificent like something trapped. Nell, he says, come quick. Nell, who is passing through the module, swims up into the dome. The two of them treading air in their lookout. The airglow is dusty greenish yellow. Beneath it in the gap between atmosphere and earth is a fuzz of neon which starts to stir. It ripples, spills, it's smoke that pours across the face of the planet; the ice is green, the underside of the spacecraft an alien pall. The light gains edges and limbs; folds and opens. Strains against the inside of the atmosphere, writhes and flexes. Sends up plumes. Fluoresces and brightens. Detonates then in towers of light. Erupts clean through the atmosphere and puts up towers two hundred miles high. At the top of the towers is a swathe of magenta that obscures the stars, and across the globe a shimmering hum of rolling light, of flickering, quavering, flooding light, and the depth of space is mapped in light. Here the flowing, flooding green, there the snaking blades of neon, there the vertical columns of red, there the comets blazing by, there the close stars that seem to turn, there the far stars fixed in the heavens, beyond them the specks that can barely be seen. By now Shaun and Chie have come, and Anton is at the window in the Russian module, and Pietro

in the lab, the six of them drawn moth-like. The orbit rounds out above the Antarctic and begins its ascent towards the north. It leaves waves of aurora in its wake. The towers collapsing as if exhausted, twitches of green on the magnetic field. The South Pole recedes behind. Roman's face is like that of a child. Ofiget, he murmurs. A wow snatched from the back of the throat. Sugoii, Chie replies, and Nell echoes it. Remember this, each of them thinks. Remember this.
Samantha Harvey: Orbital

Why is a turkey is called a turkey? It depends on where you live:
In English, they are called Turkey
In Turkish, they are called Hindi.
In Hindi, they are called Peru.
In Arabic, they are called Greek Chicken.
In Greek, they are called French Chicken.
In French they are called Indian chicken.

In Europe, nationalism is bound up with paternalism to a degree that is alien to the US experience. (Imperial Germany under Bismarck pioneered the welfare state.) The UK isn't an exception. Brexit was, in part, a bet that British people are essentially Americans in their relish for capitalism, if only the dead hand of Brussels would let them go. Well, the fifth anniversary of the formal exit is this Friday. Still no UK government has felt politically safe to cut much regulation. Even the flintiest Tory must know that, if a single day were shaved off the statutory paid leave allowance, say, there would be pandemonium, much of it among Brexit voters. To be "rightwing" in Europe and America just means different things.
    Even within the Trump government, the tech bros are at philosophical odds with the pro-worker Maga base. But at least the two camps can come together over American jingoism. What is going to glue Musk to Europe's hard right? A shared position on certain cultural issues? It doesn't seem enough to paper over such wildly different visions of the proper relationship between the individual and the state. Granted, both

sides have an interest in the paralysis or destruction of the EU: it would spare Silicon Valley a lot of regulation. But the idea that tech would get an easier ride from a fragmented, populist-led Europe could only be entertained by someone with no knowledge of, say, Le Pens economic policies over the years. The attempt to build a transatlantic club of populists isn't new. Another Trump associate, Steve Bannon tried it in the past decade. These projects tend to fall short for a reason that shouldn't need spelling out. If a movement's core idea is national assertiveness, the various branches of it around the world will almost by definition come into conflict. One nation's expansionist territorial claims affect another's. The desire of Strongman X to push his tech companies into foreign markets rubs against Strongman Y's security paranoia and amour propre. The Russo-Japanese war, Operation Barbarossa, the Sino-Soviet split: liberalism owes its survival in large part to the innate fissiparousness of those who hate it. Trump, Le Pen and the like aren't monsters on anything approaching that scale. But the principle that jingoists tend to fall out, must fall out, holds. There won't be a Nationalist International.

Not long ago, self-respecting European reactionaries almost defined themselves against the US, which they saw as both culturally imperial and culturally empty. Even in the cold war, when the alternative was communism, parts of the continental right stood aloof. At least US Republicans used to notice the snub, and mind. Now? No head of government in the EU is closer to China than Viktor Orbán of Hungary. Yet no head of government in the EU is more beloved of America's anti-China hard right. Whether this double game says more about his wiliness or the attention span of today's Republicans, it is a lesson in how differently a European populist can see geopolitics from an American.
Janan Ganesh

We have no eternal allies, and we have no perpetual enemies. Our interests are eternal and perpetual, and those interests it is our duty to follow.
Lord Palmerston.

Tiramisú has a pretty sordid history. The coffee-soaked pudding has its origins in the brothels of Treviso, where, due to its supposed aphrodisiac effects, it was used to "refuel" clients. Its original form – a cup of egg yolks mixed with sugar – was called sbattutin, which in Treviso dialect translates to the less-than-subtle "bang me". The modern name Tiramisú, which evolved after the government closed down state brothels in the late 1950s, still hints towards the dish's risqué history: it translates as "lift me up".
Silvia Marchetti: The New European

Nigel Richards is the reigning world champion of Spanish Scrabble. Just don't ask him to order a coffee in Madrid. The 57-year-old New Zealander doesn't speak the language. In his title-winning match, he racked up triple-word scores with enrugase (to wrinkle up) and enhotos (an archaic word for "familiarity"), before clinching victory with saburrosa (an obscure term that describes the coated residue of the tongue). But he didn't know what any of them meant. The word-whizz – who is also the undisputed GOAT of English Scrabble, with five world titles – simply memorised the entire Spanish dictionary. One local newspaper called his win "the height of absurdity"; a broadcaster in Madrid said it was "the ultimate humiliation". But those in the know were unsurprised. Richards had done this trick before – in French. Twice.
Richards cuts a singular figure in the Scrabbleworld, where he is known simply as Nigel – "a single, universally recognised name like Serena, Rafa, Pelé and Tiger", says Howard Warner, former head of New Zealand's Scrabble federation. Warner describes Richards's personal life as "monk-like": he is a vegetarian who lives in Malaysia, doesn't drink or smoke, has no television and shows little interest in current affairs. In addition to Scrabble, which he learnt playing with his mum in Christchurch, his only other interest is cycling, and he often rides hundreds of miles a week. A similar calm pervades his matches, and his victories. When Richards won his first English-language championship, the host asked how it felt to be

the king of Scrabble. "Nice," he replied, then took his trophy and walked off stage.
The Washington Post

To marry one actress is unfortunate. To marry two is simply asking for it.
Tom Stoppard: The Real Thing

Falsehood flies, while the truth comes limping after it.
Jonathan Swift

I'm suspicious of people who don't like dogs, but I trust a dog when it doesn't like a person.
Bill Murray

The secret to a happy marriage is creaking bed springs from laughter, not sex.
Jilly Cooper

This is from the obituary of Joe Saumarez Smith, Chair of the British Horse Racing Association who died this year aged 53.

Practical jokes, poker and negronis were three friends to Joe Saumarez Smith, only a short head behind horses. So when Martin Amis, then Britain's most fashionable novelist, attended one of his often riotous poker games, the script was written.
"Mr Amis, they tell me you're a writer," began the young Saumarez Smith, contorting his boyish face in mock ignorance, card shark that he was.
"So am I." If silence can be pictured, the room looked pretty quiet. While at the time Saumarez Smith was a junior reporter, in reality he was decidedly more modest about his literary abilities than the enfant terrible of English letters. Salman Rushdie, creased in silent laughter, stood behind a twitching Amis. Saumarez Smith kept up the barrage of ever more preposterous questions ("do you write long or short books, Martin?"), forcing the author to answer politely through gritted teeth. Unsurprisingly, over three decades Saumarez Smith's

Bloomsbury card games attracted a dedicated crowd as diverse as Ross Boatman, Victoria Coren Mitchell and the playwright Patrick Marber, who would occasionally break into song.

When choosing between two evils, I always pick the one I never tried before.
Mae West

Doveryai no proveryai (Trust but verify)
Russian proverb

People say nothing is impossible, but I do nothing every day.
AA Milne

Why it's called the Gulf of Mexico

The world cares very little about what a man or woman knows; it is what a man or woman is able to do that counts.
Virgil

The reformer has enemies in all those who profit by the old order, and only lukewarm defenders in all those who would profit by the new.
Machiavelli

Into my heart an air that kills
From yon far country blows;
What are those blue remembered hills,
What spires, what farms are those?
That is the land of lost content,
I see it shining plain,
The happy highways where I went
And cannot come again.
AE Houseman: A Shropshire Lad

Europe accounts for 7 per cent of the world's population, a quarter of its economic output and half of its social spending.
Angela Merkel

We're Americans! Do you know what that means? It means our forefathers were kicked out of every decent country in the world.
Bill Murray

Is tripe kosher? It depends on the religion of the cow.
Google AI response

That's right! Let's put an end to political correctness. The Nazi slut is right. Was this incorrect enough? I hope so!
Christian Ehring, German TV presenter, satirising the leader of the far right AFD leader Alice Weidel's opposition to political correctness.

The ideal subject of totalitarian rule is not the convinced Nazi or the convinced Communist, but people for whom the distinction between fact and fiction and the distinction between true and false no longer exist.
Hannah Arendt

Germany became Gaullist, France became British, and Britain became European.
A French diplomat after the White House shakedown of Zelensky

The poor have sometimes objected to being governed badly; the rich have always objected to being governed at all.
GK Chesterton

Think about this: any organisation whose key assets are talented or skilled people – universities, theatres, law firms, churches – don't use the word 'manager' to describe the people in charge. They call them deans, senior partners, bishops, directors or team leaders. The title of manager is only used of those who are in charge of things, not people, that is the physical or inanimate parts of the organisation: the transport, the information systems, the building. Instinctively these organisations recognise that people don't like to be 'managed' and avoid the word wherever possible.
Charles Handy: 21 Letters on Life and its Challenges

We should be careful
Of each other,
we should be kind
While there is still time.
Philip Larkin

A case of irritable vowel syndrome?
NucleusLondon on the re-re-branding of the fund manager Aberdeen from Abrdn.

You can see the computer age everywhere but in the productivity statistics.
The Solow Paradox

The customer's always right; that's why everyone likes us.
Homer Simpson

The wartime slogan Keep Calm and Carry On became such a commonplace sight in Britain more than a decade ago that it seemed as though it had become, tongue in cheek, glib and knowing, the national mission statement. The wartime public information poster carrying the slogan was everywhere for a while - on mugs and tea towels, on clothing, reprinted posters, or bowdlerised and adapted as a "meme" for birthday cards. But not during the Second World War itself. The irony is that the original poster went largely unseen at the time because after 2.45m copies were printed in the early days of the war only a few were distributed. The men at the ministry concluded that it struck the wrong tone. Too alarmist perhaps, or too patronising. Most of the posters were pulped as paper pulp was in high demand.

In 2000, a rare original was discovered rolled up at the bottom of a box of old books bought at auction by Stuart Manley, a bookseller from Alnwick. When it was framed and hung in his bookshop it attracted the admiration of customers who asked where they could buy a copy. Against the wishes of his wife, his business partner, he had 500 copies printed for sale. Since then the Manleys have sold more than 100,000 copies, with countless imitations sold by others because the poster had no copyright attached to it.
Iain Davidson

When you say you agree to a thing in principle you mean that you have not the slightest intention of carrying it out in practice.
Bismarck

It may be dangerous to be America's enemy, but to be America's friend is fatal.
Henry Kissinger

One of the penalties for refusing to participate in politics is that you end up being governed by your inferiors.
Plato

The world was at war. You couldn't go somewhere and say, 'I'm at peace and I don't fight wars.

Paddy Hemingway. The last of The Few.

Praise by name, criticise by category.
Warren Buffet

A quick death
Sir: I was surprised to read that Joel Zivot believes that 'assisted suicide is neither painless nor dignified'. As a veterinary surgeon with over four decades of experience, I have probably euthanised more than a thousand animals (dogs and cats, and during the BSE outbreak, cattle) using pentobarbital sodium. Provided that the correct dose is administered, the process is rapid. Importantly, the animal loses consciousness almost immediately (in seconds). That is followed by loss of respiratory and cardiac fanction, usually in less than a minute.
  As far as the effect of pentobarbital on humans is concerned, vets are statistically much more likely to commit suicide, and often use this drug. A close friend chose this method of ending his own life. He was discovered in his surgery, 'asleep' on the floor; there was no evidence of any agonal distress at the time of death. I have no position on assisted suicide, I can see both sides
Letter to The Times

It will shock you how much it never happened.
Don Draper in Mad Men

Do not do unto others what you would not want to have done to you.
Rabbi Hillel died 4AD

A good upbringing means not that you won't spill sauce on the tablecloth, but that you won't notice it when someone else does.

Chekov

Huawei's largest data centre in China — with over a million servers - designed to look like a European town.

I am big. It's the pictures that got small.
Norma Desmond from Sunset Boulevard

This is from Question 7 by Richard Flanagan. This year we spent a week in and around the spectacular Tasmanian rain forest - and this imagination of its eventual destruction is a dagger to the heart.

But even then the rainforest was being corroded.
Soon it will be pocked with the scattered melanomas of cattle runs, pine and eucalypt plantations, fire-scabbed here and there, to say nothing of a general, growing inanity, roads to nowhere, tourist resorts, unworked mines and crowded geo-tagged Insta sites. These though will be but small insults compared to what is coming.
    Over the following decades the rain will lessen, at first imperceptibly and then dramatically, and what remains of the rainforest will slowly start drying out and dying off. For a moment or two more though the myrtles, cicatrices weeping fern and fungi, will tower and teeter, old thespians taking a final bow made more compelling by a dramatic backdrop of still steeply wooded gullies and ridges.
    Then they will start to burn.

The intricate, myriad, miraculous relationships the sum of which is Tasmanian rainforest, a precise confusion of tree, fern, moss, fungi and microbe, of animal and bird and insect, fish and invertebrate, that might be better described as an unknown civilisation, will, along with these words, become no more than the lost jetsam of time.

A silent revolution will sweep it all away, its Robespierres and Lenins and Khomeinis a conga line of faceless CEOs, investors, economists and politicians, destroying everything in which a soul—or my own at least—could once find purpose and resonance. For a great crime there should be a great criminal, not so many so small, so immemorable.

In any case, what remains will be a wet gravel desert amidst which will be found impoundments of dead water, ash heaps and tailings dams, charred tree stumps and open-cut holes, rusting derricks and cranes and ancillary structures, bricks and corro where women once washed in the incessant rain and the cold, so much detritus mirrored in dark, toxic puddles oozing heavy metals and acid and poisons. But of that annihilated civilisation: nothing.

A masked owl, the last of its kind, its riddling face outlined with a heart and bisected by a murderer's beak, will spread its ermine spotted wings and leave the last tree, searching for a home now gone forever, chittering an imminent oblivion.

We will have arrived back on Wells's time traveller's dying beach, alone, in a dimming twilight. If I were a sculptor this would be my art: rusting machinery without purpose rising out of oily scum. People might see it as beauty or meaning. But they would be wrong. It would be what remains.

Nothing.

To avoid the risk of wrinkles, ladies should avoid exciting novels, especially late at night.
The Lady's Dressing Room. 1893

When a clown moves into a palace he doesn't become a sultan. The palace becomes a circus.
Turkish proverb

What makes equality such a difficult business is that we only want it with our superiors.
Henry Becque

The fundamental weakness of Western civilization is empathy.
Elon Musk

The death of human empathy is one of the earliest and most telling signs of a culture about to fall into barbarism.
Hannah Arendt

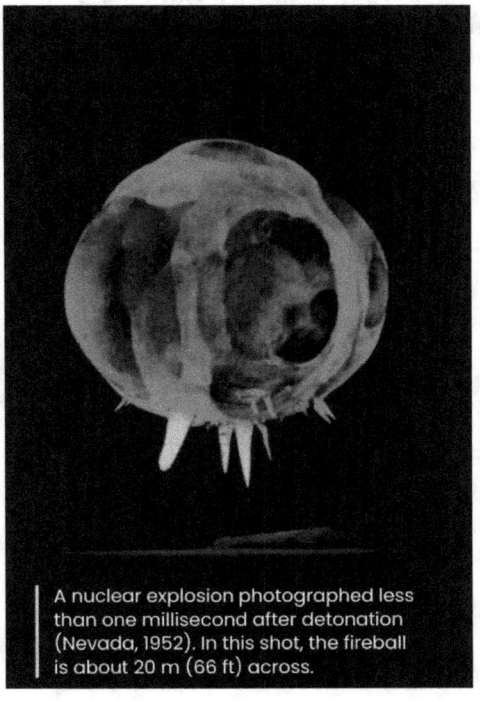

A nuclear explosion photographed less than one millisecond after detonation (Nevada, 1952). In this shot, the fireball is about 20 m (66 ft) across.

One of the best reasons for not wanting to live in the past is modern dentistry. One famous sufferer from toothache was George Washington - and if you have ever wondered why, in portraits of him, he always looks as if he's clenching his jaw - here's why.

Complete extraction begins to seem attractive, but that brings its own difficulties. Fauchard pioneered replacing lost teeth with prosthetics, and during the 18th century dentures became increasingly popular. George Washington consulted eight dentists over his lifetime and had a mouth like a battlefield. When the dental pathologist Reidar Sognnaes analysed four surviving sets of his dentures in 1976, he found teeth from elephants, hippos, walruses and cows alongside Washington's own. The dentures were used not for eating but for orating, giving shape to Washington's slurred speech. Once the spring-laden contraptions were in his mouth, he would have had to clench his jaw to stop it popping open like a jack-in-the-box. Attempts to transplant healthy teeth into diseased mouths were doomed to failure – without a root system, the transplanted tooth simply died – but some dentists still kept a stock of fresh teeth on hand for patients who requested the procedure. Often these had been 'bought' from enslaved people for a pittance; the account book from Washington's Mount Vernon plantation contains a description of one transaction for nine teeth. It's possible that such teeth made their way into Washington's own mouth, though there's no evidence to prove it.
From a review of Bite: An Incisive History of Teeth, from Hagfish to Humans
by Bill Schutt

Whatever you may be sure of, be sure of this: that you are dreadfully like other people.
James Russell Lowell

Tony Blair.
Margaret Thatcher's answer to the question of what had been her greatest success.

A society does not ever die 'from natural causes', but always dies from suicide or murder - and nearly always from the former.
Arnold Toynbee

I'll tell you what freedom means to me: no fear.
Nina Simone

The Tolkiens knew how to party

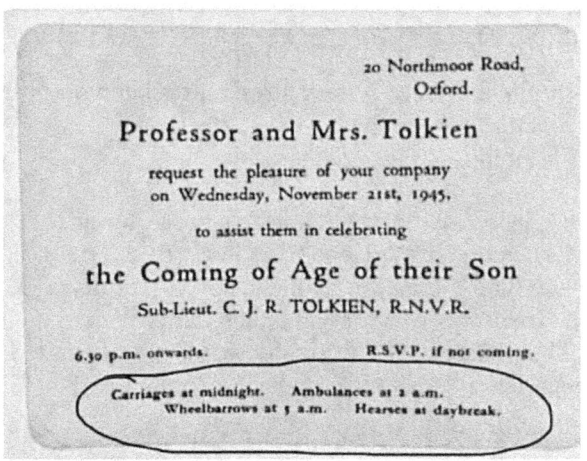

Riches should come as a reward for hard work, preferably by one's forebears.

Stephen Runciman

A cucumber should be well sliced, and dressed with pepper and vinegar, and then thrown out, as good for nothing.
Samuel Johnson

Men occasionally stumble over the truth, but most of them pick themselves up and hurry off as if nothing had happened.
Churchill

A mate of mine has just told me he's shagging his girlfriend and her twin.
I said how can you tell them apart? He said 'her brother's got a moustache!'
Billy Connelly

Those who make the worst use of their time are the first to complain of its brevity.

Jean de La Bruyère

Some circumstantial evidence is very strong, as when you find a trout in the milk.
Henry David Thoreau

The Council of Nicaea in 325AD planted the seed for an English idiom. The council's Nicene Creed said that Jesus was of "one substance with the Father", rather than of "similar substance" - in Greek this was homoousious rather than homoiousios. The difference between the words was a single i - or iota, the Greek letter - thus the expression, 'one iota of difference'.

Ventriloquize long enough and your voice alters; the mask becomes your face.
George Packer in The Atlantic on JD Vance

I do not fear death. I had been dead for billions and billions of years before I was born, and had not suffered the slightest inconvenience from it.
Mark Twain

An extraordinary affair. I gave them their orders and they wanted to stay and discuss them!
The Duke of Wellington's surprise after his first cabinet meeting as Prime Minister.

Clive James was always incongruous - a polymath, workaholic poet, writer and translator with an Aussie brawler's physique, best known as a TV presenter. This is one of his last poems.

Your death, near now, is of an easy sort.
So slow a fading out brings no real pain.

Breath growing short
Is just uncomfortable. You feel the drain
Of energy, but thought and sight remain:

Enhanced, in fact. When did you ever see
So much sweet beauty as when fine rain falls
On that small tree
And saturates your brick back garden walls,
So many Amber Rooms and mirror halls?

Ever more lavish as the dusk descends
This glistening illuminates the air.
It never ends.
Whenever the rain comes it will be there,
Beyond my time, but now I take my share.

My daughter's choice, the maple tree is new.
Come autumn and its leaves will turn to flame.
What I must do
Is live to see that. That will end the game
For me, though life continues all the same:

Filling the double doors to bathe my eyes,
A final flood of colors will live on
As my mind dies,
Burned by my vision of a world that shone
So brightly at the last, and then was gone.
Clive James: Japanese Maple

We are thus confronted with an irony of history: two centuries on, the tables have been turned. It is Europe that now cleaves closer to the Enlightenment values of secular reason, mistrust of organised faith and commitment to deliberation; the US that is in the hands of social conservatives dreaming of a return to traditional values.
Mark Mazower

The food factor should always be massive: four Bloody Marys, two grapefruits, a pot of coffee, Rangoon crepes, a half-pound of either sausage, bacon, or corned-beef hash with diced chilies, a Spanish omelette or eggs Benedict, a quart of milk, a chopped lemon for random seasoning and something like a slice of key lime pie, two margaritas and six lines of the best cocaine for dessert... Right, and there should also be two or three newspapers, all mail and messages, as well as a notebook for planning the next twenty-four hours and at least one source of good music - all of which should be dealt with outside in the warmth of a hot sun, preferably stone naked.
Hunter S Thompson's daily routine from Fear and Loathing on the Campaign Trail 1976

"It is better to have eaten something and thrown it up... and then eaten it again, than to have never eaten it at all"

- Unknown wise boi

A melancholy lesson of advancing years is the realisation that you can't make old friends.
Christopher Hitchens

These are from The Grand Encyclopaedia of Eponymous Laws

Badger's Law: Any website with the word 'Truth' in the URL has none in the posted content.

Cunningham's Law: The best way to get a correct answer to a posed question is to post the wrong answer and wait for someone to correct you.

John Gabriel's Greater Internet Fuckwad Theory: Normal Person + Anonymity + Audience = Total Fuckwad.

Munroe's Law: You will never change anyone's opinion on anything by making a post on the Internet. Knowing this will not stop you from trying.

Bradley's Bromide: If computers get too powerful, we can organize them into a committee — that will do them in.

Iron Law of Oligarchy: All forms of organisation, regardless of how democratic they may be at the start, will eventually and inevitably develop oligarchic tendencies, thus making true democracy practically and theoretically impossible, especially in large groups and complex organisations.

Lincoln's Law: If a country or group's name has the word 'People's' in it, it will have nothing to do with either democracy or The People.

Mencken's Law (a.k.a. Shaw's Law): Those who can, do. Those who cannot, teach.
- Martin's Extension: Those who cannot teach, teach education (or teach teachers; or administrate).
- Short's Extension: Those who cannot teach, criticise.
- Russell's Extension: Those who cannot teach, write.
- Some Yale Prof's Extension: Those who cannot teach, do research.
- Allen's Extension: Those who cannot teach, teach gym.

Barrow's First Law: Any universe simple enough to be understood is too simple to produce a mind able to understand it.

Benford's Law of Controversy: Passion is inversely proportional to the amount of real information available.

Box's Law: All models are wrong, but some are useful.

Clarke's 3rd Law: Any sufficiently advanced technology is indistinguishable from magic.
- Gehm's Corollary: Any technology distinguishable from magic is insufficiently advanced.
- Heterodyne's Inversion: Any sufficiently well-understood magic is indistinguishable from technology.
- Ambrose's Appendix: Any technology, no matter how primitive, is magic to those who don't understand it.

Cosmic Schmuck Principle: There are two types of people in this world: those who sometimes worry that they're a moron, and actual morons.

Goodhart's Law: When a measure becomes a target, it ceases to be a good measure

Ringwald's Law of Household Geometry: Any horizontal surface is soon piled upon.

Ruckert's Law: There is nothing so small that it can't be blown out of proportion.

Segal's Law: A man with a watch knows what time it is. A man with 2 watches is never sure.

Two Pizza Rule: If you can't feed a team with two pizzas, it's too large.

Zeigler's Law: If a politician says that government is a problem, what he means is that if you elect him, government will be a problem

'Is it summer yet' asked Pooh

'No, it's still february' said Piglet

'For fucks sake' said Pooh

Russian officials are coming up with some creative, if harebrained, schemes to encourage fertility. A Russian version of the MTV show 16 and Pregnant – which originally discouraged teen pregnancy – has been rebranded as Mum at 16, to promote it. Some regions give lump-sum bonuses to mothers who are still at school, while an education official advocated "school discos" to foster "romance for children". Other proposals include urging women to wear miniskirts, and encouraging people to "have sex during work breaks". Yes, comrade. Yes, yes, yes.
Anna Louie Sussman in The New York Times

It has been my experience that folks who have no vices have very few virtues.
Lincoln

I read this at the funeral of someone who had died with dementia. The author suffers from dementia himself and his message is both moving and educational.

When I wander, don't tell me to come and sit down.
Wander with me. It may be because I am hungry, thirsty, need the bathroom. Or maybe I just need to stretch my legs.
When I call for my mother (even though I'm ninety!) don't tell me she has died. Reassure me, cuddle me, ask me about her.
It may be that I am looking for the security that my mother once gave me.
When I shout out please don't ask me to be quiet...or walk by. I am trying to tell you something, but have difficulty in telling you what.
Be patient. Try to find out. I may be in pain. When I become agitated or appear angry, please don't reach for the drugs first. I am trying to tell you something.
It may be too hot, too bright, too noisy.
Or maybe it's because I miss my loved ones.
Try to find out first.
When I don't eat my dinner or drink my tea it may be because I've forgotten how to.
Show me what to do, remind me.
It may be that I just need to hold my knife and fork I may know what to do then.
When I push you away while you're trying to help me wash or get dressed, maybe it's because I have forgotten what you have said.
Keep telling me what you are doing over and over and over.
Maybe others will think you're the one that needs the help!
With all my thoughts and maybes, perhaps it will be you who reaches my thoughts, understands my fears, and will make me feel safe.
Maybe it will be you who I need to thank.
If only I knew how.
Norman McNamara

The only way of catching a train I ever discovered is to miss the one before.
GK Chesterton

Harrison Ruffin Tyler died this year aged 97. He was the grandson of John Tyler who was the tenth president of the USA from 1841 to 1846.

How to be a good waiter...
Always repeat the customer's order back to them (Skate sounds like 'steak' after one martini)
When waiting on someone famous, direct your conversation to others at the table, especially their spouse who will rarely receive attention in public.
Never clear a customer's coffee cup before they've left or hand them the bill before they've asked.
Don't utter the phrase 'How is everything?" (If you must break the flow of our customers' conversation, please let it be a simple 'Do you need anything?'
Never, ever, go home with a customer......for less than $500.
From restauranteur Keith McNally's memoir I Regret Almost Everything

They say never meet your heroes - but I was lucky enough to meet one of mine. James Lovelock was 101 at the time, smiling and spry as a 75 year old. His Ghia theory, in many ways, changed the way we see our planet. He was wonderfully optimistic - and this is why.

Like it or not, we're part of Gaia, and like citizens of a great nation we draw power from our membership. In common with all animals we have breathed in oxygen from plants and used it to recycle, as carbon dioxide, the food that the plants provided. Now, through our intelligence, we've allowed our planet to become aware of its environment in space and not only to see its place in the cosmos, but also to grow aware of potential threats, such as that posed by an incoming planetesimal, one of the kind believed to have ended the reign of the dinosaurs.

Because we are alive, in a rudimentary way the system has, through us, become sentient. Before this, life existed without knowing what it was, how old it was, or anything about its future. We are now travelling along a path that could lead us to become the citizens of a live, intelligent planet, which might in turn become a citizen of the galaxy. With such a future ahead of us how could we possibly be gloomy, or believe, as today's puritans keep telling us, that we are guilty of some great harm? We merely have to stop making mistakes, or better – because mistakes are inevitable – learn from them and keep our eyes on the path ahead.
James Lovelock: A Rough Ride to the Future

Kiwis lay the largest egg in relation to their body size of any species of bird in the world.

Coddiwomple v. To travel in a purposeful manner towards a vague destination.

I prefer the company of younger men. Their stories are shorter.
Dorothy Parker

Never say you know the last word about any human heart.
Henry James

Our memory is a more perfect world than the universe: it gives back life to those who no longer exist.
Maupassant

His speeches left the impression of an army of pompous phrases moving over the landscape in search of an idea; sometimes these meandering words would actually capture a straggling thought and bear it triumphantly as a prisoner in their midst, until it died of servitude and overwork.
Congressman William MacAdoo describing the rhetorical style of President Warren Harding

Roddy Llewellyn told a story about a man going into the home of two spinsters to view a Ming vase and seeing a French letter lying on the piano stool. The old lady explained: 'We found it lying on the grass on the common and it said Place on organ to avoid infection and we haven't got an organ so we put it on the piano and you know we've neither of us had any colds this year!'
From Gyles Brandreth's diaries

Where each £1 of your taxes goes
How the government spent £1.098 trillion in 2023-24

Tax description	Public sector expenditure (£bn)	
Social security (excluding state pensions)	236.3	21.6p
Health	221.0	20.2p
State pensions	124.6	11.4p
National debt interest	121.1	11.1p
Education	111.5	10.2p
Defence	56.8	5.2p
Public order and safety	47.7	4.4p
Transport	46.2	4.2p
Business and industry	45.6	4.2p
Government administration	22.8	2.1p
Housing and community amenities	19.9	1.8p
Overseas aid	7.2	0.7p
Other	34.8	3.2p

FedEx founder Fred Smith, who died on Saturday aged 80, wasn't afraid to take risks. Not long after launching the delivery business in 1973, he began to run out of money. Rather than trying to find a loan or an investor, Smith took the company's last $5,000 to a blackjack table in Las Vegas and won $27,000 – cash he used to help keep the business afloat. He said watching friends die in Vietnam had given him a different perspective. "Losing wasn't the worst thing in the world that could happen to you," he said. "I had seen that very clearly."
The Washington Post

The hype merchants are too close to the subject to see it straight. Whether or not they have a commercial incentive to talk up AI (many don't), people who devote their lives to something will naturally resist the idea that it might be of just moderate importance. At the same time, it is hard to argue against them without falling back on precedent and eternal verities. Just because most historic turning points end up being no such thing does not mean this is such a one. The AI debate often pits the informed but hysterical against the measured but generalist. Worse, we probably aren't even going to know who was right. Episodes of The Simpsons from the 1990s patronise the internet in a way that now seems mortifying. But the writers could mount a defence. Without reviving the Solow paradox ("You can see the computer age everywhere but in the productivity statistics"), US GDP growth is not higher than it was in the pre-internet decades. Much of what we do, such as travel, has changed little. The episodes, while dated, are not falsified. Here's a thought: the worst-case scenario is that AI destroys a significant but not huge share of jobs. In that world, there would be lots of victims but not enough to form an electoral plurality that could vote for universal basic income or the like. In other words, if AI sceptics are right (and the technology has a less than sweeping impact), then AI alarmists will be right (that social strife is coming). Who would have won the argument?

Janan Ganesh

Jokes from the 2025 Edinburgh Fringe

The only way most people of my generation will ever own a home is if it's left to them by their parents. We grew up with our folks saying 'I would die for my kids', and some of them are going to need to put their money where their mouth is.
Marc Jennings

My step-grandma recently called me biodiverse.
I think she meant bisexual. Or she somehow knew I had thrush.
Lulu Popplewell

Millennials' parents let a generation of kids get raised by Thomas the Tank Engine and then complain we're all autistic. What did they think was going to happen? We learnt facial expressions from trains.
Josh Elton

The NHS is in bad shape isn't it. my friend was suicidal they put him on a nine-month waiting list to a see a therapist. Luckily, in the end he got seen in 3 months. that's the great thing about being in a queue with suicidal people.
Jonny Pelham

Your dolphin may be recorded for training porpoises.
Olaf Falafel

Do you KNOW who my father is?' said a pretentious orphan.
Jamie Lee

The French are so racist, they're the only people that get angry when their football team wins a match.
Hasan Al Habib

Donald Trump is not like Hitler, Hitler served in the military. Trump is more like Bin Laden, both used their dad's money to fuck up New York's skyline.
Jena Friedman

Strategy requires thought. Tactics require observation.
Max Euwe, Dutch Chess grandmaster

War is God's way of teaching Americans geography.
Ambrose Bierce

Dilemma

The mass political movements of the 20th century were vehicles for myths inherited from religion, and it is no accident that religion is reviving now that these movements have collapsed.
John Gray

I would never die for my beliefs because I might be wrong.
Bertrand Russell

Why does TikTok benefit populists disproportionately? Because, almost by definition, populism thrives on emotions, not thoughts; on feelings not sentences. Populists specialise in providing that rush of certainty you get when you know you're right. They don't want you to think. Thinking is where certainty goes to die.
Ian Leslie

She had magnolia skin, an enchanting smile, velvet eyes, bewitching breasts, and a sinuous body softer than a krapfen alla crema. And the voice, my God! When at last they stopped dubbing it – throaty, murky, grainy – like a litany of sins. And in no way merely venial ones.
Gianfranco Angelucci on Claudia Cardinale - who died this year.

Getting old is like climbing a mountain. You get a little out of breath but the view is much better.
Ingrid Bergman

The AI revolution will make the mediocrity crisis even worse. Artificial intelligence is mediocrity memeified, magnified and mummified
Adrian Wooldridge

It's the first rule of Middle East reporting: what people tell you in private is irrelevant. All that matters is what they say in public to their own people in their own language. In Washington, officials lie in public and tell the truth in private. In the Middle East, officials lie in private and tell the truth in public.
Thomas Freidman in The New York Times

It actually doesn't take much to be considered a difficult woman. That's why there are so many of us.

Jane Goodall

He has only half learned the art of reading who has not added to it the even more refined accomplishments of skipping and skimming?
Arthur Balfour

"Things fall apart. The center cannot hold. Mere anarchy is loosed upon the world. Details at eleven."

On the anniversary of the most horrific massacre in Israel, not long after that awful atrocity at a Manchester synagogue, and seeing some clearly antisemitic elements in Saturday's rottenly timed Palestine Action rally in London, British Jews will feel raw, and I must weigh my words. But on my own behalf and on behalf - I believe - of millions of fellow citizens, including many Jews, who are deeply distressed at what has been happening in Gaza, there's something I want to say. Stop equating anger about Gaza with antisemitism.
Certainly there are antisemites who will grab any chance to vilify Jews but most of us want - and have - nothing to do with this vile minority. In online comments beneath my columns I have been called an antisemite for implying disapproval of the actions of the Israel Defence Forces. To me "antisemite" is a

dirty word. I consider it insulting in the extreme and deeply, deeply resent it being used against me and against millions like me who feel horror at what Binyamin Netanyahu's government has done in Gaza. Those who plunder the concept of antisemitism to smear opposition to slaughter and starvation are robbing a word of the terrible force it ought to have.
Matthew Parris

And when the event, the big change in your life, is simply an insight — isn't that a strange thing? That absolutely nothing changes except that you see things differently and you're less fearful and less anxious and generally stronger as a result: isn't it amazing that a completely invisible thing in your head can feel realer than anything you've experienced before? You see things more clearly and you know that you're seeing them more clearly. And it comes to you that this is what it means to love life, this is all anybody who talks seriously about God is ever talking about. Moments like this.
Jonathan Franzen: The Corrections

More people plug into the grid all the time. A quarter of a century ago, fewer than 4.5 billion people enjoyed access to electricity; that number has since risen to 7.3 billion, encompassing 91 per cent of the world's population. Hannah Ritchie, Pablo Rosado, and Max Roser from Our World in Data point out that every day since the dawn of the new millennium, more than 300,000 people on average gained access to electricity for the first time. Every. Single. Day.
Tim Gregory: Going Nuclear. How the atom will save the world

The end of October is a bad time for dyslexics - it's when their cocks go black.

Courage is the only virtue you can't fake.
Nicholas Taleb

AI is giving us the power to answer the most difficult of questions. But how do you ask the right questions? This where human imagination and intuition come in.

You have to sniff out what the right direction is, what the right experiment is, what the right question is. So picking the right question is the hardest part of science and making the right hypothesis. And that's what today's AI systems definitely can't do. I often say it's harder to come up with a really good conjecture than it is to solve it. So we may have systems soon that can solve pretty hard conjectures ... like a maths Olympiad problem. But could a system come up with a conjecture worthy of study, a really deep question? That is a far harder type of creativity. Today's systems clearly can't do that. And we're not quite sure what that mechanism would be.
Demis Hassabis: CEO of Google DeepMind and Nobel Prize winner

A student asked anthropologist Margaret Mead what marked civilisation's first sign. Expecting fishhooks or clay pots, the student was surprised when Mead said: a healed broken femur. In nature, a broken leg means death—you can't escape danger, reach water, or hunt. No animal survives long enough to heal. A healed femur proves someone stayed with the fallen, bound the wound, carried them to safety, and tended them through recovery. Helping someone through difficulty is where civilisation starts.

The real measure of your wealth is how much you'd be worth if you lost all your money.
Rabbi Hillel. Died 4AD

www.ingramcontent.com/pod-product-compliance
Lightning Source LLC
Chambersburg PA
CBHW052120070526
44584CB00017B/2576